JUST JESUS
Over 100 Verses
of the Exact Words of Jesus
Practical, Day-to-Day Wisdom
for Everyone.

A Study Guide of Just the
Words of Jesus

Created & Arranged By
"Perfect In One Moment's" Brother Steve
©2017

Meet Jesus

You can know someone by their words... so do you know the words of Jesus.

Let me introduce Jesus to you by his own words.

It will take you less than an hour to read Jesus' most popular verses. Over 100 verses from Jesus that will open your eyes and heart to the original lessons of love, truth and life. Just his words, no commentary, no opinions, no preaching... Just his words.

His quotes are organized in subject order so it reads as if Jesus himself were in front of you, one-on-one, teaching you his wisdom and love.

It does not matter if you are a Christian, Jew, Buddhist, Hindu, Muslim or even athetosis, His words go beyond religion. The practical day-to-day teachings will make you better brother, sister, father, mother, friend and neighbour.

"And there are also many other things which Jesus did, the which, if they should be written every one, I suppose that even the world itself could not contain the books that should be written." Amen.
John 21:25

In the beginning was the Word...

Thousands of years ago mankind began to talk in sophisticated language. Language so powerful that ideas, concepts, formulas, abstract thoughts began. These powerful thoughts could be turned into words and words into working objects; from metal plows to modern machines, from buildings to spaceships, computers to cell phones; unlimited achievements.

"By the word of the Lord were the heavens made, their starry host by the breath of his mouth"... "For he spoke, and it came to be; he commanded, and it stood firm".

The Word, we take for granted, formed our modern world.

A "Perpetual Miracle" the power of the Word. Even today with all our knowledge there is no other known living intelligence that can communicate in intricate thoughts conjured up by words. And everyone has to agree, it is miraculous the unending amount of imagination and creativity we have as humans. It is awesome!

And God said, "Let us make man in our image, after our likeness."

But just as awesome, and undeniable — man's relationship with God can be traced right back to the Word. What a coincidence? Traced to the Old Testament, the greatest intellectual discovery of all times, the Word.

Are our words just a language of practicality and survival, or are they more? Is our language, the Word, the direct link to our souls? Direct link to Love? The direct link to God and the Holy Spirit? Even in our thoughts, we talk to ourselves in words.

The Old Testament describes the Word as: Creative, good, holy, complete, flawless, all-sufficient, sure, right and true, understandable, active, all-powerful, indestructible, supreme, eternal, life-giving, wise, and trustworthy.

Another coincidence? Around two-thousand years ago Jesus was born. And just a miraculous and significant, God in the book of John said, "And the Word was made flesh, and dwelt among us, full of grace and truth." Meet Jesus.

Jesus' words are the most powerful words ever spoken. There is no other person, even today, that influences and inspires as many people as Jesus.

There are over two billion Christians worldwide. Jesus' words were the beginning of our struggle for true freedom; His words are even echoed in our Constitution. Jesus' words even though they seem to be steeped in religion are actually practical Words of wisdom. Wisdom on how to love each other, the Will of God and how to be "Perfect in One" John 17:-21-23.

A Moment with Moses

The sand blasting around, the wind howling, the air dry but cool and refreshing. In the distance a speck of undulating bright light. Circling around, getting closer to the light, on the east a midnight blue sky, stars and planets shining through like bright pin holes. In the west, a sunset on the distant desert horizon; revolving around the light, getting closer and closer, brighter and brighter.

A burning plant, a bush of fire, the branches danced like liquid flames made of intriguing elements. Words, symbols, universes, atoms, molecules; infinite moving intelligent pieces, sounds, voices, music, a thunderous explosion of wonder… And then frozen time.

Instantly stopped in the power of the Light - voices singing, talking in cadence repeating, I am, I am, "Tell them I am that I am". Words spoke in deep voices, soft voices, children's voices, all different languages of the world, totally surrounded by the words…

"I am, That I am." God

In the beginning was the Word,
and the Word was with God,
and the Word was God.
John 1:1

And the Word was made flesh, and
dwelt among us, full of grace and truth.
John 1:14

And God said, Let us make man in
our image, after our likeness.
Genesis 1:26

And Jesus said:

The words that I speak unto you,
they are spirit, and they are life.
John 6:63

You shall know the truth and
the truth will make you free.
John 8:32

For the Creator, God is a Spirit.
John 4:24

NOTES AND INSPIRATIONS

Believe in God in the Spirit and in truth, for
they are the believers God seeks.
God is spirit, and his believers must worship
and live in the Spirit and in truth.
John 4:24

The wind blows where it wishes,
and you hear the sound of it, but cannot tell
where it comes from and where it goes.
So is everyone who is born again of the Spirit.
John 3:8

No one can enter the kingdom of God
unless they are born again of water and the Spirit.
John 3:5

That which is born of the flesh is flesh; and
that which is born of the Spirit is spirit.
John 3:6

You should not be surprised at my saying,
You must be born again.
John 3:7

Unless you repent you will all
likewise perish.
Luke 13:3

NOTES AND INSPIRATIONS

I am the Alpha and Omega,
the beginning and the end.
Revelations 1:8

I am the way, the truth, and the life.
John 14:6

I am the Son of Man.
John 3:13

I am the Son of God.
John 10:36

In me there is life,
and the life was the light of men.
John 1:4

If anyone hears my words, and does not believe, I judge you not: for I came not to judge the world, but to save the world.
John 12:47

I came not to call the righteous,
but sinners to repentance.
Luke 5:32

NOTES AND INSPIRATIONS

For the Son of Man is come
to save that which was lost.
Matthew 18:11

Come unto me, all ye that labour and
are heavy laden, and I will give you rest.
Matthew 11:28

Take my yoke upon you, and learn of me;
for I am meek and lowly in heart:
and ye shall find rest unto your souls.
Matthew 11:29

For my yoke is easy, and my burden is light.
Matthew 11:30

Suffer little children, and forbid them not,
to come unto me:
for of such is the kingdom of heaven.
Matthew 19:14

And whoso shall receive one such little
child in my name receiveth me.
Matthew 18:15

And you should become as little children
to enter into heaven.
Matthew 18:3

NOTES AND INSPIRATIONS

Whosoever therefore shall
humble himself as a little child,
the same is greatest in the kingdom of heaven.
Matthew 18:4

And he that shall humble himself
shall be exalted.
Matthew 23:12

Blessed are the poor in spirit:
for theirs is also the kingdom of heaven.
Matthew 5:3

Blessed are they that mourn:
for they shall be comforted.
Matthew 5:4

Blessed are the meek:
for they shall inherit the earth.
Matthew 5:5

Blessed are they which do hunger and thirst
after righteousness: for they shall be filled.
Matthew 5:6

Blessed are the merciful:
for they shall obtain mercy.
Matthew 5:7

Blessed are the pure in heart:
for they shall see God.
Matthew 5:8

NOTES AND INSPIRATIONS

Blessed are the peacemakers: for they shall
be called the children of God.
Matthew 5:9

Blessed are they are persecuted for righteousness' sake: for theirs is the kingdom of heaven.
Matthew 5:10

Blessed are they that have not seen,
and yet have believed.
John 20:29

Blessed are they that hear the
Word of the Creator, and keep it.
Luke 11:28

For I hungered, and ye gave me food:
I was thirsty, and ye gave me drink:
I was a stranger, and ye took me in:
Naked, and ye clothed me:
I was sick, and ye visited me:
I was in prison, and ye came unto me.
Inasmuch as ye have done it unto one of
the least of these my brethren, ye have
done it unto me.
Matthew 25:35-40

Give and it will be Given to You.
Luke 6:38

NOTES AND INSPIRATIONS

If you knew the gift of God, and who it is that asks you for a drink, you would have asked him and he would have given you living water.
John 4:10

Everyone who drinks the water of this world will be thirsty again, but whoever drinks the living water I give you will never thirst. Indeed, the water I give them will become in them a spring of water welling up to eternal life.
John 4:13-14

He that believes on me out of his belly shall flow rivers of living water.
John 7 7:38

So he who loves Me will be loved by God, and I will love him and manifest Myself to him.
John 14:21

NOTES AND INSPIRATIONS

I have called you friends; for all things that I have heard of my Father I have made known unto you.
John 15:15

I am the vine, you are the branches: You that abides in me, and I in him, the same bring forth much fruit: for without me ye can do nothing.
John 15:5

That we may be one; as God is in me, and I in you, that they also may be one in us. And the glory which thou gave me I have given them; that they may be one, even as we are one: I in them, and thou in me, that they may be made...

Perfect in One.
John 17:21-23

NOTES AND INSPIRATIONS

Rejoice in his light.
John 5:35

If a you walk in the night, you will stumble, because there is no light in you.
John 11:10

If you walk in the day, you will not stumble, because you see the light of this world.
John 11:9

Light has come into the world, but you loved darkness instead of light because your deeds are evil and sinful. Everyone who does evil hates the light, and will not come into the light for fear that their deeds will be exposed.
John 3:19-21

I am the light of the world:
he that followeth me shall not walk in darkness, but shall have the light of life.
John 8:12

I have come as a light into the world, that whoever believes in Me should not abide in darkness.
John 12:46

NOTES AND INSPIRATIONS

But whoever lives by the truth comes into the light, so that it may be seen plainly that what they have done and their deeds has been done in the sight of God.
Matthew 11:28

As long as I am in the world,
I am the Light of the world.
Matthew 11:28

If then your whole body is full of light, having no part dark, the whole body will be full of light, as when the bright shining of a lamp gives you light.
Matthew 11:28

In me there is life,
and the life was the Light of men.
Matthew 11:28

That was the true Light, which gives light to everyone coming into the world.
John 1:9

NOTES AND INSPIRATIONS

The light of the body is the eye: therefore when thine eye is good, thy whole body also is full of light; but when thine eye is evil, thy body also is full of darkness.
Matthew 6:22

So let your light so shine before men, that they may see your good works, and glorify God, the creator which is in heaven.
Matthew 5:16

While you have the light, believe in the light, that you may become children of light.
John 12:36

NOTES AND INSPIRATIONS

This is my commandment, That ye love
one another, as I have loved you.
Greater love hath no person than this, that
a you lay down his life for your friends.
John 15:12-13

Thou shalt love one another
as you love yourself.
Matthew 22:39

But I also say to you, love your enemies, bless
those who curse you, do good to those who
hate you, and pray for those who spitefully
use you and persecute you, that you may be
children of God the Creator in heaven.
Matthew 5:44

So Judge not less you be judged:
For with what judgment you judge, you
shall be judged: and with what you measure, it shall be measured to you again.
Matthew 7:1-2

For you are without sin among us, let
them first cast a stone at your brothers
and sisters for there sins.
John 8:7

NOTES AND INSPIRATIONS

You ask, How often shall I let another sin
against me, and I forgive them? Seven times?
I say not unto thee, seven times?
But, forgive them seventy times seven.
Matthew 18:21-22

Therefore do not worry, saying,
'What shall we eat?' or 'What shall we
drink?' or 'What shall we wear?'
Matthew 6:31

Therefore I say to you, do not worry about your life...
Is not life more than food
and the body more than clothing?
Matthew 6:25

Can any one of you by worrying add a
single hour to your life ?
Matthew 6:27

Consider the lilies of the field, how
they grow: they neither toil nor spin;
If then God so clothes the grass, which
today is in the field and tomorrow is

NOTES AND INSPIRATIONS

thrown into the oven, how much
more will the Creator clothe you.
Matthew 6:28

Look at the birds of the air, for they neither
sow nor reap nor gather into barns;
yet your heavenly Creator, God feeds them.
Are you not of more value than they?
Matthew 6:26

And fear not them which kill the body,
but are not able to kill the soul:
but rather fear him which is able to destroy
both soul and body.
Are not two sparrows sold for a few dollars?
And one of them shall not fall on the
ground without your Father.
Fear ye not therefore, ye are of more value
than many sparrows.
But the very hairs of your head are all numbered.
Matthew 10:28-30

And when you are delivered up to testify,
do not worry beforehand, or premeditate
what you will speak. But whatever is given
you in that hour, speak that; for it is not
you who speak, but the Holy Spirit.
Mark 13:11

NOTES AND INSPIRATIONS

Take therefore no thought for the tomorrow:
for the tomorrow shall take thought for
the things of itself.
Matthew 6:34

And when you pray…

If ye abide in me, and my words abide in
you, ye shall ask what ye will,
and it shall be done unto you.
John 15:7

And when you pray, don't pray standing in the
churches and in the corners of the streets loud
and boastful that everyone will notice you.
Matthew 6:5

But you pray, enter into thy closet, and
shut the door, pray to God which is in secret;
and God which seeth in secret shall
reward thee openly.
Matthew 6:6

NOTES AND INSPIRATIONS

And all things, whatsoever ye shall ask in prayer, believing, ye shall receive.
Matthew 21:22

But when ye pray, use not vain repetitions, as the non believers do: for they think that they shall be heard for their much speaking.
Be not like them: for God knows what things you have need of, before you ask him.
Matthew 6:7-8

After this manner therefore pray:
Our Father which art in heaven,
Hallowed be thy name.
Thy kingdom come, Thy will be done in earth, as it is in heaven.
Give us this day our daily bread.
And forgive us our sins,
as we forgive those who have sinned against us.
And lead us not into temptation,
but deliver us from evil:
For thine is the kingdom, and the power, and the glory, for ever.
Matthew 6:9-13

NOTES AND INSPIRATIONS

For if ye forgive others their trespasses, your heavenly Father will also forgive you:
But if ye forgive not others their trespasses, neither will your Father forgive your trespasses.
Matthew 6:15

And why worry about the speck that is in your brother's eye, When you are blinded by the beam is in your own eye?
First cast out the beam out of your own eye; and then shalt thou see clearly to cast out the speck of dust out of thy brother's eye.
Matthew 7:4-5

Ye have heard that it hath been said, An eye for an eye, and a tooth for a tooth:
But I say unto you, That you resist not evil: but whosoever shall hit you on thy right cheek, turn to him the other also.
Matthew 5:38-39

And if any man will sue thee at the law, and take away your coat, let him have your cloak also.
Matthew 5:40

NOTES AND INSPIRATIONS

And whosoever shall compel you to go
a mile with them, go with him
two miles.
Matthew 5:41

Give to them that ask you, and from
them that would borrow of you
do not turn away.
Matthew 5:42

Ye have heard Thou shalt not kill; and whosoever shall kill shall be in danger of the judgment.
Matthew 5:21

But I say unto you, That whosoever is angry
with another without a cause shall be in
danger of the judgment.
Matthew 5:22

Ye have heard Thou shalt not commit adultery:
But I say unto you, That whosoever looks on a
another to lust hath committed adultery
already in their heart.
Matthew 5:27-28

NOTES AND INSPIRATIONS

You shall love God the Creator with all your heart, and with all your soul, and with all your mind.
Matthew 22:37

But I say unto you, Swear not at all; neither by heaven; for it is God's throne.
Matthew 5:34

Nor by the earth; for it is his footstool:
Matthew 5:35

Neither shalt thou swear by thy head, because thou can not make one hair white or black.
Matthew 5:36

NOTES AND INSPIRATIONS

Lay not up for yourselves treasures upon earth,

But lay up for yourselves treasures in heaven, where neither moth, nor rust doth corrupt, and where thieves do not break through nor steal: For where your treasure is, there will your heart be also.
Matthew 6:20-21

For what shall it profit a man, if he shall gain the whole world, and lose his own soul?
Mark 8:36

Because strait is the gate, and narrow is the path, which leadeth unto life, and few there be that find it.
Matthew 7:14

Go and sell that thou hast, and give to the poor, and thou shalt have treasure in heaven: and come and follow me.
Matthew 19:21

NOTES AND INSPIRATIONS

Repent:
for the kingdom of heaven is at hand.
Matthew 4:17

Ask and it will be given to you;
seek and you will find;
knock and the door will be opened to you.
Matthew 7:7

I am the door:
by me if any man enter in, he shall be saved,
and shall go in and out, and find eternal life.
John 10:9

Therefore whosoever hears my words,
and doeth them, I will liken him unto a wise
man, which built his house upon a rock:
And the rain descended, and the floods came,
and the winds blew,
and beat upon that house; and it fell not:
for it was founded upon a rock.
Matthew 7:24-25

These things have I spoken unto you, that my
joy might remain in you, and that your
joy might be full.
John 15:11

NOTES AND INSPIRATIONS

For where two or three are gathered together in my name, there am I in the midst of them.
John 15:15

Peace be unto you: as God hath sent me, even so send I you.
Luke 24:36

For God, our Creator, so loved the world, that he gave his only begotten Son, that whosoever believes in him should not perish, but have everlasting life.
John 3:16

Peace I leave with you, my peace I give unto you: not as the world gives, give I unto you. Let not your heart be troubled, neither let it be afraid.
John 14:27

Teaching them to observe all things whatsoever I have commanded you: and, lo, I am with you always, even unto the end of the world.
Matthew 28:20

Go, and sin no more.
John 8:11

NOTES AND INSPIRATIONS

It is God who gives you the true bread from heaven. For the bread of God is the bread that comes down from heaven and gives life to the world.
John 6:32-33

This is the bread that came down from heaven.
John 6:41

I am the bread of life. Whoever comes to me and believes will never go hungry, and whoever believes in me will never be thirsty.
John 6:35

I am the living bread that came down from heaven. Whoever eats this bread will live forever.
This bread is my flesh,
which I will give for the life of the world.
John 6:51

For my flesh is real food
and my blood is real drink.
Whoever eats my flesh and drinks my blood remains in me, and I in them.
Matthew 6:55-56

NOTES AND INSPIRATIONS

Just as the living God sent me and I live because of the God, so the one who feeds on me will live because of me.
John 6:57

I have given them the Word; and the world hath hated them, because they are not of the world, even as
I am not of the world.
John 17:14

Sanctify them through thy truth: thy Word is truth.
John 17:17

Follow me; and let the dead bury their dead.
Matthew 8:22

The harvest truly is great, but the labourers are few; Pray ye therefore the Lord of the harvest, that he will send forth labourers into his harvest.
Luke 10:2

NOTES AND INSPIRATIONS

JUST JESUS
Over 100 Verses
of the exact Words of Jesus
practical, day-to-day wisdom for everyone.

QR Code Study Guide
of Just the Words of Jesus

QRC - Quick Response Code Section
Use your cell phone to share the Words of Jesus, by scanning these inspiring verses and sending them to friends, family, neighbours and coworkers.

QR Codes are best read in bright light, however due to the code or scanner the QR Code may not scan, just try again until your optical scanner reads the QR Code.

In the beginning was the Word, and the Word was with God, and the Word was God.
John 1:1

I am the Alpha and Omega, the beginning and the end.
Revelations 1:8

And the Word was made flesh, and dwelt among us, full of grace and truth.
John 1:14

I am the way, the truth, and the life.
John 14:6

And God said, Let us make man in our image, after our likeness.
Genesis 1:26

The words that I speak unto you, they are spirit, and they are life.
John 6:63

NOTES AND INSPIRATIONS

For the Creator, God is a Spirit.
John 4:24

In me there is life, and the life was the light of men. - *John 1:4*

I am the Son of Man. - *John 3:13*

If anyone hears my words, and does not believe, I judge you not: for I came not to judge the world, but to save the world.
John 12:47

I am the Son of God. - *John 10:36*

I came not to call the righteous, but sinners to repentance. - *Luke 5:32*

NOTES AND INSPIRATIONS

For the Son of man is come
to save that which was lost.
Matthew 18:11

For my yoke is easy, and my burden is
light. *Matthew 11:30*

Come unto me, all ye that labour and are
heavy laden, and I will give you rest.
Matthew 11:28

Suffer little children, and forbid them not,
to come unto me: for of such is the kingdom
of heaven. *Matthew 19:14*

Take my yoke upon you, and learn of me;
for I am meek and lowly in heart:
and ye shall find rest unto your souls.
Matthew 11:29

And whoso shall receive one such little
child in my name receiveth me.
Matthew 18:15

NOTES AND INSPIRATIONS

And you should become as little children to enter into heaven.
Matthew 18:3

Blessed are the poor in spirit: for theirs is also the kingdom of heaven.

Blessed are they that mourn: for they shall be comforted.

Blessed are the meek: for they shall inherit the earth.

Blessed are they which do hunger and thirst after righteousness: for they shall be filled.

Blessed are the merciful: for they shall obtain mercy.

Blessed are the pure in heart: for they shall see God.

Blessed are the peacemakers: for they shall be called the children of God.

Blessed are they are persecuted for righteousness' sake: for theirs is the kingdom of heaven. *Matthew 5:3-10*

Whosoever therefore shall humble himself as a little child, the same is greatest in the kingdom of heaven. *Matthew 18:4*

And he that shall humble himself shall be exalted. *Matthew 23:12*

NOTES AND INSPIRATIONS

Blessed are they that have not seen,
and yet have believed.
John 20:29

Give and it will be Given to You.
Luke 6:38

Blessed are they that hear the
word of the Creator, and keep it.
Luke 11:28

If you knew the gift of God and who it is that asks you for a drink, you would have asked him and he would have given you living water. - *John 4:10*
Everyone who drinks this water of this world will be thirsty again, but whoever drinks the living water I give you will never thirst. Indeed, the water I give them will become in them a spring of water welling up to eternal life. - *John 4:13-14*

For I hungered, and ye gave me food:
I was thirsty, and ye gave me drink:
I was a stranger, and ye took me in:
Naked, and ye clothed me:
I was sick, and ye visited me:
I was in prison, and ye came unto me.
Inasmuch as ye have done it unto one of the least of these
my brethren, ye have done it unto me.

Matthew 25:35-40

NOTES AND INSPIRATIONS

He that believeth on me out of his belly shall flow rivers of living water.
John 7:38

No one can enter the kingdom of God unless they are born again of water and the Spirit. *John 3:5*

Believe in God in the Spirit and in truth, for they are the believers God seeks. God is spirit, and his believers must worship and live in the Spirit and in truth.
John 4:24

That which is born of the flesh is flesh; and that which is born of the Spirit is spirit. *John 3:6*

The wind blows where it wishes, and you hear the sound of it, but cannot tell where it comes from and where it goes. So is everyone who is born again of the Spirit. *John 3:8*

You should not be surprised at my saying, You must be born again.
John 3:7

NOTES AND INSPIRATIONS

Unless you repent you will all likewise perish. *Luke 13:3*

That we may be one; as God is in me, and I in you, that they also may be one in us. And the glory which thou gavest me I have given them; that they may be one, even as we are one: I in them, and thou in me, that they may be made perfect in one;
John 17:21-23

So he who loves Me will be loved by God, and I will love him and manifest Myself to him. *John 14:21*

I am in God, as He is in me and I am in you.

I am the vine, you are the branches: You that abides in me, and I in him, the same bring forth much fruit: for without me ye can do nothing.
John 15:5

Rejoice in his light. - *John 5:35*

NOTES AND INSPIRATIONS

If a you walk in the night, you will stumble, because there is no light in you.
John 11:10

I am the light of the world: he that followeth me shall not walk in darkness, but shall have the light of life. *John 8:12*

If you walk in the day, you will not stumble, because you see the light of this world. *John 11:9*

I have come as a light into the world, that whoever believes in Me should not abide in darkness. *John 12:46*

Light has come into the world, but you loved darkness instead of light because your deeds are evil and sinful. Everyone who does evil hates the light, and will not come into the light for fear that their deeds will be exposed. *John 3:19-21*

But whoever lives by the truth comes into the light, so that it may be seen plainly that what they have done and their deeds has been done in the sight of God.
Matthew 11:28

NOTES AND INSPIRATIONS

As long as I am in the world,
I am the light of the world.
Matthew 11:28

That was the true Light, which gives light
to everyone coming into the world.
John 1:9

If then your whole body is full of light,
having no part dark, the whole body will
be full of light, as when the bright shining
of a lamp gives you light. *Matthew 11:28*

The light of the body is the eye:
therefore when thine eye is good, thy
whole body also is full of light; but when
thine eye is evil, thy body also is full of
darkness. *Matthew 6:22*

In me there is life, and the life was the
light of men. *Matthew 11:28*

So let your light so shine before men, that they
may see your good works, and glorify God, the
creator which is in heaven. *Matthew 5:16*

NOTES AND INSPIRATIONS

While you have the light, believe in the light, that you may become children of light. *John 12:36*

You shall love God the Creator with all your heart, and with all your soul, and with all your mind. *Matthew 22:37*

You shall know the truth and the truth will set you free. *John 8:32*

Thou shalt love one another as you love yourself. *Matthew 22:39*

This is my commandment, That ye love one another, as I have loved you. Greater love hath no person than this, that a you lay down his life for your friends. *John 15:12-13*

But I also say to you, love your enemies, bless those who curse you, do good to those who hate you, and pray for those who spitefully use you and persecute you, that you may be children of God the Creator in heaven. *Matthew 5:44*

NOTES AND INSPIRATIONS

So Judge not less you be judged:
For with what judgment you judge, you shall be judged: and with what you measure, it shall be measured to you again.
Matthew 7:1-2

Therefore do not worry, saying, 'What shall we eat?' or 'What shall we drink?' or 'What shall we wear?'
Matthew 6:31

For you is without sin among us, let him first cast a stone at your brothers and sisters for there sins. *John 8:7*

Therefore I say to you, do not worry about your life, what you will eat or what you will drink; nor about your body, what you will put on. Is not life more than food and the body more than clothing? *Matthew 6:25*

You ask, How often shall I let another sin against me, and I forgive them? Seven times? I say not unto thee, seven times? But, forgive them seventy times seven.
Matthew 18:21-22

Can any one of you by worrying add a single hour to your life? *Matthew 6:27*

NOTES AND INSPIRATIONS

Consider the lilies of the field, how they grow: they neither toil nor spin; If then God so clothes the grass, which today is in the field and tomorrow is thrown into the oven, how much more will the Creator clothe you.
Matthew 6:28

And fear not them which kill the body, but are not able to kill the soul: but rather fear him which is able to destroy both soul and body. Are not two sparrows sold for a few dollars? And one of them shall not fall on the ground without your Father. Fear ye not therefore, ye are of more value than many sparrows. But the very hairs of your head are all numbered.
Matthew 10:28-30

Look at the birds of the air, for they neither sow nor reap nor gather into barns; yet your heavenly Creator, God feeds them. Are you not of more value than they?
Matthew 6:26

And when you are delivered up to testify, do not worry beforehand, or premeditate what you will speak. But whatever is given you in that hour, speak that; for it is not you who speak, but the Holy Spirit.
Mark 13:11

NOTES AND INSPIRATIONS

Take therefore no thought for the tomorrow: for the tomorrow shall take thought for the things of itself. *Matthew 6:34*

But you pray, enter into thy closet, and shut the door, pray to God which is in secret; and God which seeth in secret shall reward thee openly. *Matthew 6:6*

If ye abide in me, and my words abide in you, ye shall ask what ye will, and it shall be done unto you. *John 15:7*

And all things, whatsoever ye shall ask in prayer, believing, ye shall receive. *Matthew 21:22*

And when you pray, don't pray standing in the churches and in the corners of the streets loud and boastful that everyone will notice you. *Matthew 6:5*

But when ye pray, use not vain repetitions, as the non believers do: for they think that they shall be heard for their much speaking. Be not like them: for God knows what things you have need of, before you ask him. *Matthew 6:7-8*

NOTES AND INSPIRATIONS

After this manner therefore pray:
Our Father which art in heaven,
Hallowed be thy name.
Thy kingdom come, Thy will be done in earth, as it is in heaven.
Give us this day our daily bread.
And forgive us our sins, as we forgive those who have sinned against us.
And lead us not into temptation, but deliver us from evil:
For thine is the kingdom, and the power, and the glory, for ever.
Matthew 6:9-13

And why worry about the speck that is in your brother's eye, When you are blinded by the beam is in your own eye?
First cast out the beam out of your own eye; and then shalt thou see clearly to cast out the speck of dust out of thy brother's eye.
Matthew 7:4-5

Ye have heard that it hath been said, An eye for an eye, and a tooth for a tooth: But I say unto you, That you resist not evil: but whosoever shall hit you on thy right cheek, turn to him the other also.
Matthew 5:38-39

For if ye forgive others their trespasses, your heavenly Father will also forgive you:
But if ye forgive not others their trespasses, neither will your Father forgive your trespasses.
Matthew 6:15

NOTES AND INSPIRATIONS

And if any man will sue thee at the law, and take away your coat, let him have your cloak also. *Matthew 5:40*

Ye have heard Thou shalt not kill; and whosoever shall kill shall be in danger of the judgment. *Matthew 5:21*

And whosoever shall compel you to go a mile with them, go with him two miles. *Matthew 5:41*

But I say unto you, That whosoever is angry with another without a cause shall be in danger of the judgment. *Matthew 5:22*

Give to them that ask you, and from them that would borrow of you do not turn away. *Matthew 5:42*

Ye have heard Thou shalt not commit adultery: But I say unto you, That whosoever looketh on a another to lust hath committed adultery already in their heart. *Matthew 5:27-28*

NOTES AND INSPIRATIONS

But I say unto you, Swear not at all; neither by heaven; for it is God's throne. Nor by the earth; for it is his footstool: Neither shalt thou swear by thy head, because thou canst not make one hair white or black. *Matthew 5:34-36*

For what shall it profit a man, if he shall gain the whole world, and lose his own soul? *Mark 8:36*

Lay not up for yourselves treasures upon earth, But lay up for yourselves treasures in heaven, where neither moth, nor rust doth corrupt, and where thieves do not break through nor steal: For where your treasure is, there will your heart be also. *Matthew 6:20-21*

Because strait is the gate, and narrow is the path, which leadeth unto life, and few there be that find it. *Matthew 7:14*

NOTES AND INSPIRATIONS

Go and sell that thou hast, and give to the poor, and thou shalt have treasure in heaven: and come and follow me.
It is God who gives you the true bread from heaven. For the bread of God is the bread that comes down from heaven and gives life to the world. *Matthew 19:21*

I am the living bread that came down from heaven. Whoever eats this bread will live forever. This bread is my flesh, which I will give for the life of the world. *John 6:51*

I am the bread of life. Whoever comes to me and believes will never go hungry, and whoever believes in me will never be thirsty. *John 6:35*

Unless you eat the flesh of the Son of Man and drink his blood, you have no life in you. Whoever eats my flesh and drinks my blood has eternal life, and I will raise them up. *John 6:53-54*

NOTES AND INSPIRATIONS

For my flesh is real food and my blood is real drink. Whoever eats my flesh and drinks my blood remains in me, and I in them. *Matthew 6:55-56*

I have given them the Word; and the world hath hated them, because they are not of the world, even as I am not of the world. *John 17:14*

Just as the living God sent me and I live because of the God, so the one who feeds on me will live because of me. *John 6:57*

Sanctify them through thy truth: thy Word is truth. *John 17:17*

This is the bread that came down from heaven. *John 6:41*

Repent: for the kingdom of heaven is at hand. *Matthew 4:17*

NOTES AND INSPIRATIONS

I am the door: by me if any man enter in, he shall be saved, and shall go in and out, and find eternal life. *John 10:9*

These things have I spoken unto you, that my joy might remain in you, and that your joy might be full. *John 15:11*

Ask and it will be given to you; seek and you will find; knock and the door will be opened to you. *Matthew 7:7*

But I have called you friends. *John 15:15*

Therefore whosoever hears my words, and doeth them, I will liken him unto a wise man, which built his house upon a rock: And the rain descended, and the floods came, and the winds blew, and beat upon that house; and it fell not: for it was founded upon a rock. *Matthew 7:24-25*

For where two or three are gathered together in my name, there am I in the midst of them. *John 15:15*

NOTES AND INSPIRATIONS

Peace be unto you: as God hath sent me, even so send I you.
Luke 24:36

Go, and sin no more. *John 8:11*

For God, our Creator, so loved the world, that he gave his only begotten Son, that whosoever believes in him should not perish, but have everlasting life. *John 3:16*

Teaching them to observe all things whatsoever I have commanded you: and, lo, I am with you always, even unto the end of the world. *Matthew 28:20*

Peace I leave with you, my peace I give unto you: not as the world giveth, give I unto you. Let not your heart be troubled, neither let it be afraid. *John 14:27*

The harvest truly is great, but the laborers are few; Pray ye therefore the Lord of the harvest, that he will send forth labourers into his harvest.
Luke 10:2

NOTES AND INSPIRATIONS

NOTES AND INSPIRATIONS

NOTES AND INSPIRATIONS

NOTES AND INSPIRATIONS

NOTES AND INSPIRATIONS

NOTES AND INSPIRATIONS

Made in the USA
Columbia, SC
17 January 2019